Introducing design in embroidery

Introducing design in embroidery

Betty Chicken

B T Batsford Limited

I dedicate this book to my husband, Harry, and my son, Stephen, without whose encouragement it would not have been written.

First published 1971
7134 2648 9

Filmset by Keyspools Limited   Golborne   Lancashire
Printed and bound in Denmark by
F E Bording Limited   Copenhagen
for the publishers
B T Batsford Limited
4 Fitzhardinge Street   London W1

Contents

Acknowledgment

I should like to thank the following:
The children of Hill Top County Middle and Infants' School, Burslem, Stoke-on-Trent, for working some of the items photographed; the headmaster, Mr R. Scholes, who encouraged me to experiment and gave me every facility to do so; the Chief Education Officer for Stoke-on-Trent, Mr H. Dibden, MA, BSc, FRSA, for permission to use the children's work; Mrs Jean Carter, NDD, ATC, ATD (Manchester), Lecturer in Embroidery at Eastbourne College of Education and free-lance artist, for permission to use photographs of her work and for passing on to me her enthusiasm for the subject; Miss Alice V. White, Senior Lecturer in Crafts at St Katherine's College of Education, Liverpool, for her encouragement and practical advice; Miss Anne Butler, Head of the School of Embroidery, Manchester Polytechnic, for her permission to use photographs of her own work and that of her students; Miss Constance Howard, Mrs Joy Clucas, Mrs Vera Sherman, Miss Dorothy Gandevia, Miss Beryl Chapman, Miss Mary Goldizen and Mrs Eirian Short for permission to use photographs of their work; the heads of Dalston County Secondary School, London E 8, Channing School, Highgate, Baylis Court County Secondary School, Slough and the Grammar School for Girls, Cleethorpes for permission to use photographs of girls' work; the Embroiderers' Guild for permission to use their photographs of *Oodles* and *Safari*.

Church Lawton, Stoke-on-Trent 1970   B.C.

End papers are a detail from *Intern* panel by Beryl Chapman.

Introduction

Creative embroidery is interpreted as being a mixture of art and embroidery. It could be defined as embroidery designed and worked by the artist who uses a needle, thread and fabric instead of a brush, paint and paper. Unfortunately many teachers fail to see embroidery in this light and in primary schools particularly the use of embroidery is often restricted to a few rows of stitches on an apron or traycloth.

The principles of basic design, which are now taught in art classes, can be applied when using fabrics and threads. It is the modern trend to leave children to choose their own topic and medium in the art class, allowing them to express themselves freely and to develop their own styles. When they reach the ages of eleven, twelve and thirteen they can be introduced to the principles of basic design.

A brief definition of basic design could be designing from the absolute basics of drawing, the point and the line, and the shapes developed from them. Colour and texture are other basic requirements for a composition. While agreeing with the necessity for freedom of choice—I find children do produce better work if they choose their own subjects and medium—there are times when it is possible to work with one group on a particular aspect of design. Through discussion and suggestion, ideas can be formulated and exchanged and the children's work benefits from this.

The aim of this book is to show how fabrics and threads can be used in the primary school as an art medium, incorporating simple embroidery and collage techniques and following the principles of basic design. It does not set out to be a comprehensive scheme of work but offers suggestions which could stimulate other ideas in the reader's mind. Some of the work illustrated was done by nine, ten and eleven year old children. Other work was by younger and older boys and girls, students and artist-craftsmen.

1 Point

When the children and I first began to talk about point and line I tried to explain to them how these were the basic 'shapes' from which all other shapes developed. Or conversely, all shapes could be reduced to a point or line. In order that they should understand clearly, I asked them to imagine they were looking at a city from the top of a tall building. Photographs taken from church towers or other high buildings were useful here. It was noted how the buildings below were still recognisable. Then we imagined we had boarded an aeroplane and had taken off and climbed high into the sky. Now the city below was hardly recognisable. Roads had become lines of varying widths and blocks of buildings had become rectangles, or squares. Continuing our imaginary flight we noticed that isolated buildings were mere dots, sometimes roundish, other times squarish. So we had an example of how large shapes can be reduced in size to their basic point or line.

Looking through books we observed group formations in nature . . . fish swimming in a shoal, frogspawn clinging together in a pond, primroses growing in a clump, shells scattered on a seashore, birds flying in formation and disease marks on leaves. In our minds we translated these into points on a background and noticed the distribution of these points. When we came to experiment with point designs we were able to look back on these observations and use them as sources of design.

Design experiments

Our first experiments produced a variety of results, depending as much on the distribution of the points as on the means of producing them. Some points were round, some square and some irregular. Some were larger than the others. The points were in rows, or scattered freely, or in groups in definite areas. Some designs were made of only one size of point, others had been made of points of various sizes. Some children's designs just grew from nothing, while others had been inspired by the nature books, and the points were grouped like their sources of inspiration.

After discussing the variations in our experiments, we saw that not only was the position of the point important in relation to the other points, but also in relation to its background.

For these first experiments we used drawing materials, printing materials, paper fasteners, coloured card discs, stars, buttons, sequins, beads, mineral bottle tops and apple and melon seeds. At this preliminary stage we used black and white colours or one other colour on a contrasting background in order to emphasise the relationship between point and point and between point and background, and so avoid at this time any decision having to be made on colour and texture.

The following details give some of the variations possible on the theme of frogspawn. One child simply cut out circles of plain and patterned fabrics and stuck them onto a card background so that each circle overlapped its neighbour. Another child padded her shapes and sewed them to the background fabric. Her original overlapping circles were given a stencil-like treatment. A group of girls cut out and decorated felt circles and added weed-like curved lines to complete the composition. Another group made rosettes using a patterned fabric and plain fabrics taken from its colour scheme. They secured these to the background and added beads to the centres and stitchery to the background.

Suggestions for experiment

The following suggestions for experiments can be adapted for use with children of various ages and abilities. The simplest idea can be carried out by seven-year-olds and yet the same idea can be taken by an older child and treated in a different manner.

Remember, these are only suggestions. Innumerable variations are possible for each one, depending on the choice of fabric, thread, colour, texture and technique of application and decoration.

Using points of the same size, attach them in regular rows. Add interest by choice of colours. For example, from one particular point vary the tones outwards from light to dark, or dark to light. Or try another suggestion—decide on a certain number of colours, not the same number as points in the row, and repeat them regularly. Experiment with a patchwork background.

Create a design of points in rows by using piano music notes without their stems. Find inspiration from the full scores of orchestral works, operas and musicals.

Arrange points of the same size in rows, then remove so many of them at random until a pleasing arrangement is obtained. Try a patterned fabric background with plain dots.

Make a completely free design of similar sized points placed at random.

Group together points of similar size and join the groups together with more points.

Scatter the points so that there are areas of varying density.

Experiment with these former suggestions using points of different sizes.

The point can be represented by a hole. Cut out holes in a piece of non-frayable material and attach to another background fabric.

Sources of inspiration

Modern art
Natural groupings—shells on the shore
Lighted windows at night
Computer tape patterns
Micrographs of metals
Diatoms
Stars in the sky
Crystals.
Collect and display pictures
    showing point distribution.

Overleaf
2 The background has been divided into areas of varying tonal density. Point and line effects have been achieved by the use of beads, sequins, rings, fabrics and threads
Dorothy Kavanagh, Embroidery School, Manchester Polytechnic

1 Point designs

2

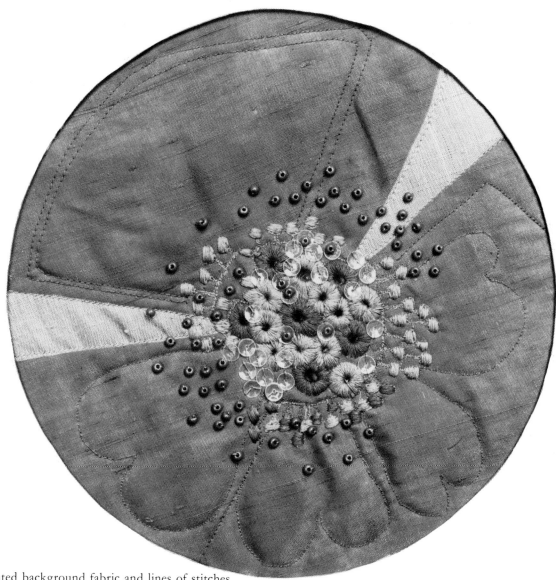

3   The printed background fabric and lines of stitches
give the impression of a flower. Points in the central area
are formed by eyelets, sequins, beads and straight stitches
Angela Senior, Embroidery School, Manchester Polytechnic

4 Holes were cut in red felt and the fabric was then attached to a black and white patterned Tricel background
Patricia Miller, Hill Top County Middle and Infants' School, Burslem

2 Line

Through practical experiments with pen, pencil, crayon, paint, chalk, charcoal, paper cutting and printing, the children found that lines could be long, short, straight, curved, thick, thin, vertical, horizontal and diagonal. They could cross each other and meet each other at various angles and in various places.

From there it was an easy step to introduce fabrics and threads and explore their possibilities. Ribbons, braids, strips of felt and other non-frayable fabrics, tape, binding, wool and string were used successfully. Paste secured most fabrics to either a card or fabric background. Threads were immersed in the paste and used when squeezed out. This ensured complete contact.

Designing with fabrics and threads

First experiments need only be in black and white or in a limited colour scheme, but further designs can be more ambitious colourwise and texturally. Although these exercises are primarily concerned with line, colour and texture should not be completely ignored. I try to teach the children to repeat to themselves 'form, colour and texture,' whenever and whatever they are designing.

The following suggestions can be used in many ways. In their simplest form they can be straightforward exercises. But they can become attractive designs depending on the pattern of the lines, the combination of colours used and the variety of texture produced. Some of the ideas can be worked on a large scale by a group of children. Other designs can be deliberately cut into sections to be worked, then re-assembled like a jig-saw.

Suggestions for designs can be discussed before commencing on a particular type of experiment. (See *Sources of inspiration* page 17.)

Experiments can be carried out using:

(a) two colours. One will be for the background and the other for the fabric or thread. Choose colours of different tone, ie light and dark. (See Chapter 6: Colour.) Remember to make the texture differences interesting, eg shiny threads on a matt background;

(b) textured threads of one colour on a contrasting background. Some could be smooth or rough, tightly or loosely spun, hairy or silky, knobbly, knotted or slub. Thin or thick threads could be used or make your own by twisting or plaiting. (See Chapter 7: Texture)

(c) a limited number of colours. (See Chapter 6: Colour.) Do not forget about texture;

(d) a number of fabrics. Vary colour and texture. (See appropriate chapters)

(e) fabrics and threads. Plan a definite colour scheme at the start and also decide on areas of differing textures;

(f) surface stitches.

Suggestions for experiment

Using groups of threads make a design of straight or curved lines. This could be a border-type design or an all-over pattern.

Place an imaginary or real obstacle in the path of the lines, forcing the lines to alter course. This obstacle could be a patch of fabric of contrasting or toning colour, or merely an area of the background left empty.

In various places make a line drawing in thread of a natural or geometrical shape. Continue these lines horizontally or vertically to the edges.

Cut felt or other fabric in curves of varying thickness. Attach these to the background either with the pieces spaced at intervals or close together.

Fill in a recognisable shape, eg fish, butterfly, bird, with straight or curved lines using one or more fabrics or threads.

Take a line for a walk. Try Paul Klee's suggestion using threads.

Calligraphy. The formation of letters, not only of our own alphabet, but of others too, lends itself to design possibilities. Investigate Russian, Chinese, Sanskrit, Hebrew and Greek.

Pictorial compositions. Children's line drawings can be adapted for use with threads.

Mathematical type of designs. Use threads stretched between paper fasteners, beads, points of a circle, etc.

Fabric destruction. By drawing out threads from a fabric, line designs can be created.Withdraw at regular or irregular intervals single or groups of threads. Alter the angle of the remaining threads by tying or stitching. Fray edges and arrange by tying or plaiting or encourage them to lie in a certain direction.

Stretch strong threads across a wooden frame. Create a design by weaving different textured fabrics and threads through the web.

Sources of inspiration (Also see Chapter 4)

Kandinsky's paintings
Railway lines—aerial photographs of large junctions can provide useful source material
Motorways—aerial photographs again are useful, particularly of the large intersections found in the USA and Japan
Maps—roads, rivers, contours
Markings on birds and butterflies
Bookshelf arrangements
Telegraph posts and wires
Electricity pylons
Lamp posts
Rock strata
Flower petals
Grass and corn: partly-cut cornfield
Scaffolding and tubular steel constructions.

Think of others yourself. Make a collection of pictures from magazines and display and discuss them from the design point of view.

5   Line designs

6

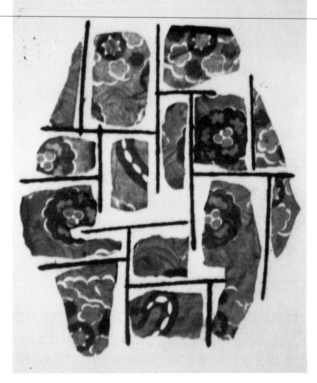

7

6   Line designs using threads

7   T-junction design. An area of the background was masked and T-junction lines were drawn in thread. The 'spaces' created were partially filled with patterned fabric Janice Bloor, Hill Top County Middle and Infants' School, Burslem

Facing page
8   Mary Hunt, Grammar School for Girls, Cleethorpes

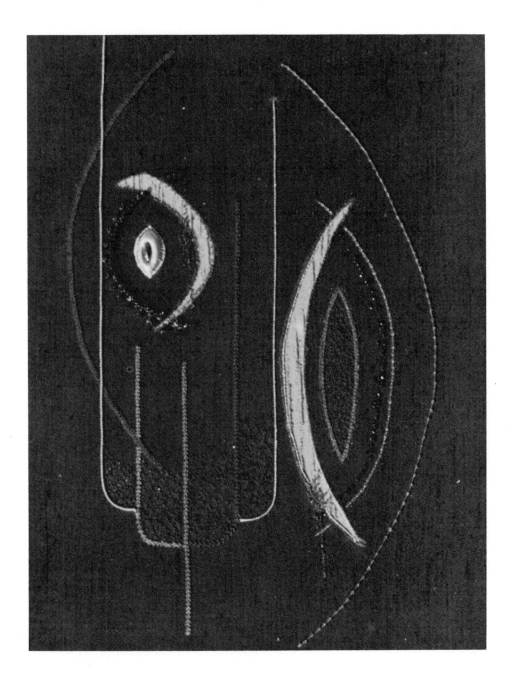

9 *Green Gloaming* Joy Clucas

10   Canvas work exercise
Patricia Miller, Hill Top County Middle and Infants'
School, Burslem

11 *Gold Strata* Joy Clucas

12   Various methods of embroidery have been used in
this panel
Dorothy Kavanagh, Embroidery School, Manchester
Polytechnic

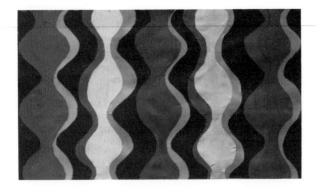

13

14

15

24

16   Diane Gratty, Hill Top County Middle and Infants' School, Burslem

13   A curved line design was drawn. The solid areas were traced, cut out of fabric and stuck onto the background
Richard Groom, Hill Top County Middle and Infants' School, Burslem

14   Three curved lines were drawn then filled with letters. The background was made from two pieces of patterned fabric, one patterned red and the other green. The letters were traced and cut out of black felt
Susan Thompson, Hill Top County Middle and Infants' School, Burslem

15   A rectangle of hessian was frayed, then tied to resemble a multi-legged insect. Sequins add interest
Janet Barnett, Hill Top County Middle and Infants' School, Burslem

17   *Rainbow in the Sky*   Eirian Short

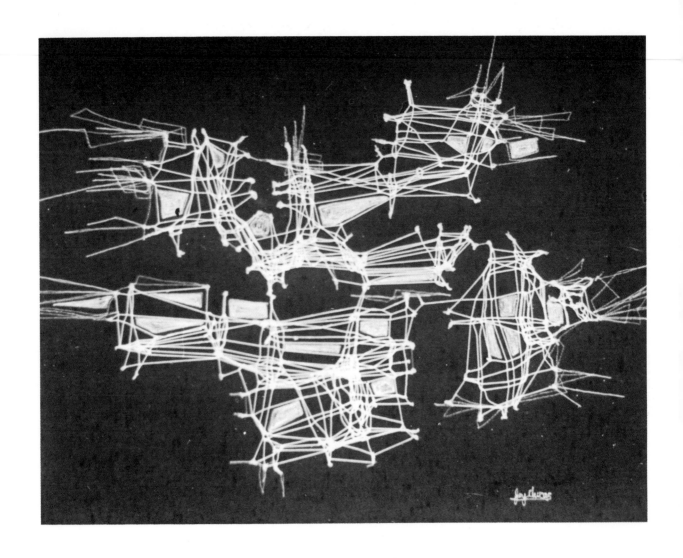

18 *White Structure* Joy Clucas

3 Geometric shapes

In Chapter 2 we were concentrating on line and evolving designs composed of lines. Where these lines met to create shapes we were aware of these shapes but did not emphasise them as it was with line that we were experimenting and we pushed these shapes into the background.

If we now consider these shapes made from joining together a certain number of lines we find they are geometrical.

Children derive a great deal of pleasure from designing with regular geometrical shapes, whether they are breaking them down or using many of them to create a new shape.

Experiment with the following ideas using squares, circles, triangles, hexagons, rectangles or any other geometrical shape. In addition to the suggestions for adapting designs into fabrics and threads found in Chapter 2, try working out these ideas in canvas work, drawn fabric or patchwork.

Suggestions for experiment

Divide a square or rectangle into a number of smaller squares or rectangles of equal size.

Using one zigzag line and one curved line, make a design on the outer edges of a square, rectangle or hexagon. Join a number of these together closely or a little apart to form a larger shape. Decide which area is to be the background and which the foreground.

Divide the square, rectangle or hexagon into squares, rectangles and/or hexagons. Arrange a number of these shapes to form a larger design.

Devise a mathematical formula to divide the square or rectangle. For example a shape 1524 mm (6 in.) wide could be divided vertically in the proportions 3 : 1 : 2. Repeat this shape a number of times, and assemble them in a pleasing manner to form a larger design. Decide which is the background and which is the foreground.

Mark out a square, rectangle or diamond into a pre-determined number of squares, rectangles or diamonds. Cut along the lines, altering direction. Assemble a number of these to form a larger design.

Explode a square or circle. Rearrange the pieces leaving gaps between them.

Cut up squares, circles or triangles into concentric or solid shapes. Rearrange all or some of them to create a design.

Draw a number of concentric circles inside a circle. Create an Op Art design using lines pointing in various directions. Interpret in beads, stitches and appliqué.

Fill in a geometrical shape with long irregular-shaped pieces of fabric, all radiating from one point. Vary colour and texture.

Fold a circle in half. Cut out a central circle. Draw and cut out a design based on curved lines. Use fabrics and/or threads to work the resulting design.

Cut out numerous rings in light and medium transparent fabrics. Place on a dark background and stretch threads under, through and over them, radiating from one point off-centre.

Fill a square with squares. Collage techniques could be used with embroidery stitches and appliqué.

Arrange a number of transparent circles, triangles, etc. to make a pleasing design. Add texture in certain areas.

Draw a design of squares, triangles and rectangles on a half-circle. Reverse the design on the other half and alter the colour emphasis.

Draw a number of off-centre concentric circles. Draw lines radiating from the middle of the centre circle. Repeat a design in each segment. Use applique and decorate with stitches etc. Vary the colour and texture.

Draw a free design within the limits of a geometrical shape.

Area division

The rectangle or square is often the frame within which a design is composed. Apart from a completely free design within these limits there are a number of mathematical methods of dividing an area which are useful to know, as they could be used on a large scale for group work. The divided rectangle or square can be cut up to be worked by several children then reassembled as a whole.

Dancing Squares Constance Howard. By courtesy of
Stoke-on-Trent Education Committee

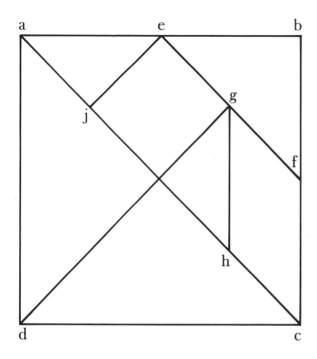

1 The Chinese Tangram. These shapes can be cut out and rearranged to form patterns or figures. To construct a tangram draw a square abcd. Join ac. Find point e (ae = eb). Find point f (bf = fc). Join ef. Draw the line dg along the imaginary diagonal db. To find gh half the right-angle fgd. To find ej draw a right-angle at e meeting ac at j.

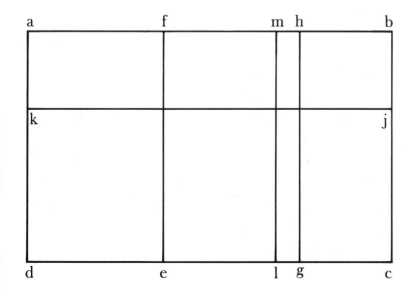

2 Draw any rectangle abcd.

de = ad	$\angle fed$ = 90°
eg = de	$\angle hge$ = 90°
gc = cj	$\angle kjc$ = 90°
el = lc	$\angle mlc$ = 90°

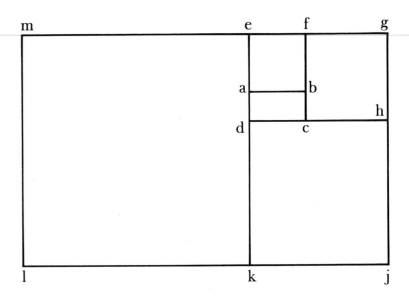

3 Build up from a small rectangle abcd.
   Draw a square abfe on ab
   Draw a square fchg on fc
   Draw a square dhjk on dh
   Draw a square eklm on ek.
Repeat to required size.

4 Conversely, beginning with the rectangle mgjl. Join gl. Draw a line from j to meet gl at 90°. Extend this line to mg at e. From e drop a perpendicular line to k on lj. Repeat this in rectangle egjk. ej is the diagonal. From d drop a perpendicular line to h on gj. Repeat this in rectangle cghd. bg is the diagonal. From c drop a perpendicular line to f on eg. Repeat this in rectangle efcd. From b drop a perpendicular to a on ed.

Sources of inspiration

Modern art
Floor and wall tile designs
Snowflakes
Architectural plans
Coffee cup top bubbles
Photographs of buildings, views, etc (an automatic square or rectangular frame)
Cross sections of spherical fruit and vegetables
Cross sections of stems, twigs, branches and trunks
Photomicrographs of radiolaria
Jewellery
Mosaics
Islamic architectural detail.

Collect and display exhibits and pictures which could come under the heading *Designs using geometrical shapes.*

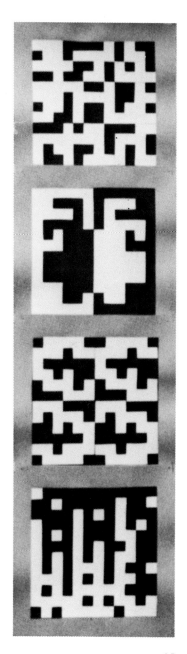

20 Designs based on the square

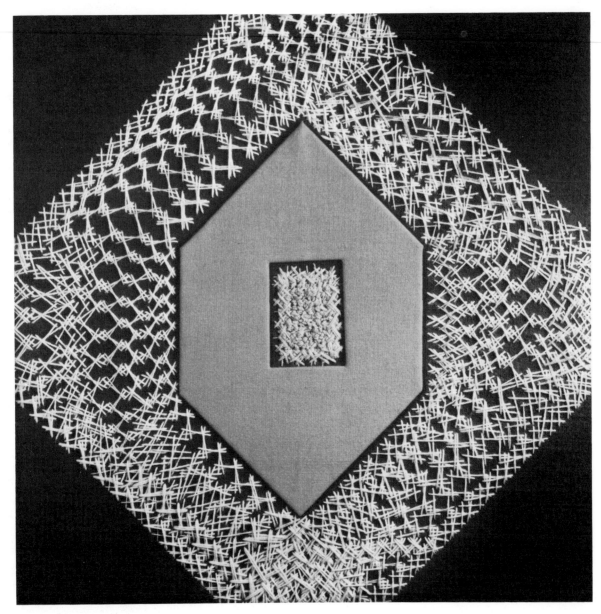

21 *Enlargement* Anne Butler

22 *Three Diamonds* Anne Butler

23 A kneeler
Carol Blackburn, Embroidery School, Manchester Polytechnic

24 *Box of Sweets* Eirian Short

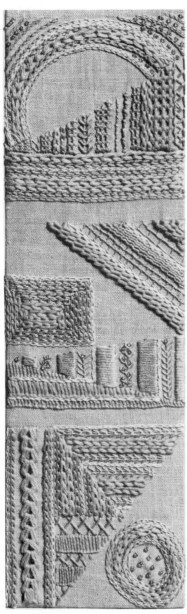

25 *Three squares* Betty Chicken

26 Lynn Mulhall, Embroidery School, Manchester Polytechnic

Facing page
27 Commissioned abstract hanging by Joy Clucas

28   *Blues City*   Jean Carter

4 Free shapes and sources of inspiration

The term *free shapes* covers everything which is not geometrical and includes abstract design, figures and topics from nature. The range of possible subjects is very wide but it is astounding to find how few are actually chosen as the sources of inspiration.

The next few paragraphs are directed primarily towards the teacher or adult, but the knowledge acquired, if the suggestions are assimilated, will be transmitted to the children.

Collecting design examples

It is useful to keep a scrapbook or box file of pictures which appeal for some reason. This attraction may be connected with colour or texture or design. Colour and texture will be discussed in later chapters. We concentrate on design in this one.

Learn to see design everywhere. If possible, make actual notes, not mental ones, of items which catch your eye through the day.

Make photostat copies of pictures in books which might be useful.

Take off-beat photographs of ordinary objects from an unusual angle, such as scrap in a junkyard, builders' waste material on a building site, stacks or rows of objects in a factory yard.

Occasionally make a deliberate effort to collect pictures of a certain subject not very well covered in your collection, as the human tendency is to collect only a few topics towards which one is unconsciously biased.

Take an ordinary everyday object which does not seem particularly inspiring and make a simple drawing of it. Make patterns with the shape. Keep them, together with a sketch of the original object.

Visit art and crafts exhibitions at museums, galleries and colleges. Keep their catalogues for future reference.

Cut out pictures from magazines of items awarded prizes for good design, for the principles of good design are basic to all art and crafts.

Take photographs, make sketches or buy postcards of items of interest in your area which give your region its character. Similarly, when visiting other parts of the country, or countries abroad, collect visual evidence of their characteristics. Some obvious differences are building materials—patterns of brickwork or stonework—style and proportions of buildings—patterns of roofs, windows, tiles, doors, chimneys, towers, spires, porches—industrial building designs, oasthouses, windmills, pottery kilns, pithead structures, cooling towers, dockland cranes—the skyline—the line of the coast, the shape of cliffs, the grouping of objects, animate and inanimate, on the beach—field and hill shapes.

Design sources

To the adult many subjects in nature seem hackneyed, repeated time and time again with a slight variation. But these same subjects can be new to children and they can approach the subject with enthusiasm. Such things as flowers, leaves, fruit, vegetables, insects, butterflies, birds, fish, sea life, animals, etc, can be used as subjects, either singly or in groups.

Photomicrographs of scientific subjects can be extremely interesting from the design point of view. These highly magnified photographs show us patterns in such things as metals and crystals that are almost unbelievable.

Geographical subjects lend themselves particularly to abstract design. Landscapes and aerial photographs of many different types of features provide interesting patterns. Maps showing contours, county boundaries, crop distribution, islands, etc. can be used.

In history, civilian, military and ecclesiastical costumes both ancient and modern, domestic furniture and furnishings, methods of transport, etc can be adapted for the purposes of design. Museum visits reveal interesting items.

Churches of many religions provide beautiful examples of design both outside and inside. Stonework, mosaics, tapestries, carved wood, wrought ironwork, stained glass, murals, frescoes, arches, ceilings, roofs, towers, minarets, statues, crosses, sculptures of contemporary as well as older styles can be the basis for design. Signs and symbols of different faiths and religious festivals can inspire design.

Less obvious subjects like music and games need not be overlooked. The lines, curves and forms of many instruments are inspiring, and games equipment, including chessmen, skittles and tennis racquets all have shapes which can be used to create design.

30   Jill Martin, Channing School, London N 6

29   Mary Hunt, Grammar School for Girls, Cleethorpes

32 *Moth against the Moon* Eirian Short

Facing page
31 *Safari* One of four panels from this school which were awarded the Senior Cup in the 1969 Embroiderers' Guild Schools' Competition
Jane Torbett, Baylis Court Secondary School, Slough

Overleaf
33 *Knight on Horseback* Vera Sherman. Designed and worked especially for a child. One of a series worked by the artist on the theme of horses

33

Stone   Constance Howard

34 *Swan in the Sunset*   Eirian Short

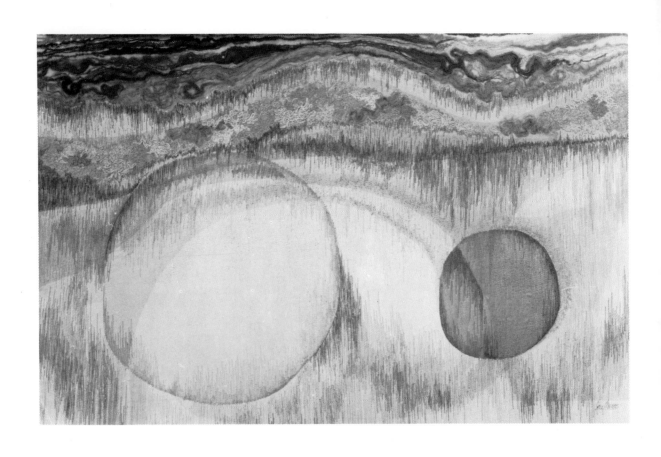

35 *Red Rain* Joy Clucas

36 *Maelstrom* Joy Clucas

37 *Busy City* Jean Carter

38 *Three Kings* Highly Commended in the Embroiderers' Guild Schools' Competition, Senior Section, 1969
Briar Brownson, Channing School, London N6

40 *The Envious Circusmaster* Group work, Hill Top
County Middle and Infants' School, Burslem

Facing page
39 *A Christmas King* Flowers and leaves were cut from
a patterned fabric and applied to the background with
couched wool. The body, based on a rectangle of
patterned furnishing fabric, was decorated with Gold-
fingering wool. The velvet head-dress had an applied
patterned motif added with beads and rings attached and
gold fringe and braid for additional splendour
Susan Thompson, Hill Top County Middle and Infants'
School, Burslem

41   Radio Telescope, Jodrell Bank

43 and 44   Design sources from tree trunks and coal

42   Little Moreton Hall, Cheshire

Designs can be found in local buildings. Metal structures are composed of lines and joined lines create shapes. Tudor buildings have many black and white patterns on them. Sketches can be collected to form the basis of a design.

45 and 46   Construction and destruction. A building site and the demolition of a wrecked vessel provide many interesting shapes and lines

47 and 48   The natural groupings of flowers, leaves and fruit can inspire design

Adapting a design from a photograph or object

In spite of all these suggestions, there may still be confusion as to how to use these ideas for designing an embroidered panel.

First we must ask ourselves what is our aim. Is the panel to be an abstract or a pictorial composition? What shape and size of frame is required? Having decided these points, we are ready to adapt the topic accordingly.

Look at the photograph or object and decide what it is that appeals to you. Is it the direction of certain lines? Is it the positioning of particular shapes? Is it the distribution of tonal values? Is it the variety of texture? Having decided, draw a simplified sketch of the photograph or object, emphasising the points which appealed to you.

Now forget about the original source of inspiration and consider the design as a number of lines and shapes to be coloured and given texture.

If the design is to be a pictorial composition, again simplify the drawing. Figures can be based on geometrical shapes. Some amusing as well as attractive figures can emerge from triangles and circles!

Having completed the drawing and put away the source of inspiration it is time to decide how to decorate the design. The aim of this is that the finished work should be decorative, not realistic. If a realistic effect is wanted, then, in my opinion, embroidery is not the medium to use. So natural colours need not be used, and realistic textures such as fur for animals and real hair for figures should be avoided.

The finished fabric collage or embroidery may not look like the original source of inspiration but this is not important. The photograph or object is only the starting point.

In the classroom, encourage the children to bring articles of a specified shape and display them together with pictures. Discuss pictures from the point of view of design. Is the picture composed of lines, points or shapes? The children will soon be pointing out to the teacher examples of these. My nine-year-old son recently handed me a bunch of 'points and lines'. They were fir cones and spiky pine leaves.

5 Three-dimensional and kinetic work

Work in three-dimensions is possible with children. Some of the suggestions are easy, others more difficult and only suitable for the more able children.

Shape givers

Some sort of shape-giver or shape-raiser is necessary in this type of work. The shape can be stuck or sewn to the background, depending on the weight and the background.

Thick card, expanded polystyrene, tiles or plywood can be covered with fabrics or threads and attached to a solid background by a block of light-weight balsa wood or a bobbin.

Layers of thick fabric such as felt or heavyweight woollen cloth can be used as padding.

Shapes with depth need a solid foundation to support the sides. A block of wood, particularly light-weight balsa wood, a thick piece of foam rubber or layers of polystyrene tiles could be used. The fabrics can be stuck to or sewn round the shapes.

Plastic washing-up liquid bottles can be cut up and covered then sewn onto the background. A stiffened belt foundation could also be used.

Boxes, cartons and tins can be used four ways—open side at the front, open-side at the back, open-side at the top or open-side at the bottom.

Strips of card or stiffener can be covered and sewn down with the protruding part in a curve or bent to create a triangle or a square. The same sort of strip can be sewn on edgeways.

Expanded polystyrene spheres can be decorated. Half or whole ones can be used.

Kinetic work can be made. Shapes hanging from certain points will move slightly in a draught, particularly if they are positioned slightly in front of the background.

Shapes can be attached to the background in such a way that it is possible to turn them and so change the design.

Deep boxes can be used to create suspended displays of decorated shapes at various depths.

Mobiles can be made from fabrics and threads.

Sculpture-like designs can be created on a standing base. Cane or thick wire could be used for the framework.

Constructions can be built up from various shapes added to each other ad infinitum.

Fashions and styles are constantly changing in the art world and it is useful to be aware of these. Visits to exhibitions bring them to one's notice. Many ideas worked out in other crafts can be adapted—repeat—adapted (not copied) for use with fabrics and threads.

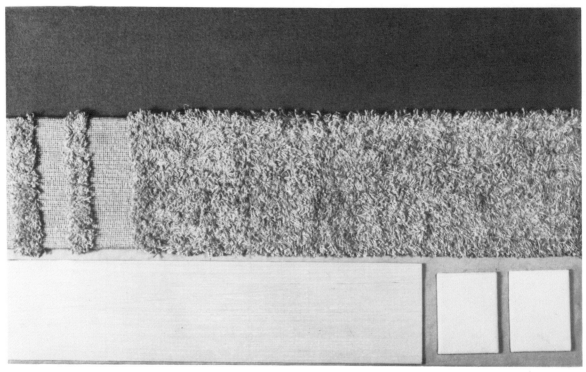

49 *Direction* Anne Butler

Facing page
50 *Oodles* Cup winner in Advanced Section of the Embroiderers' Guild Schools' Competition, 1969
Lesley Hogger, Dalston County Secondary School, London E.8

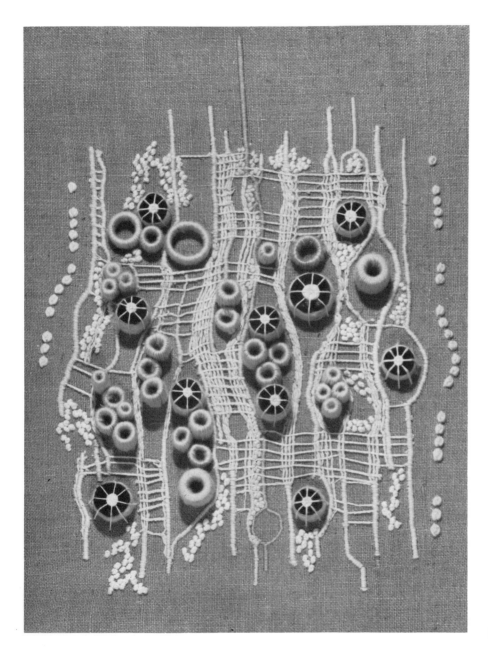

50

6 Colour

Choice of colour is a very personal matter. A scheme which appeals to one person may not impress another. Psychologists tell us we express our characters in our choice of colours. So it is possible for a person to be very conscious of slight variations of tone in certain colours but not as sensitive to tonal differences in others. A more scientific method of choosing colours is to refer to a colour wheel.

Primary and secondary colours

Primary colours—red, yellow and blue—do not contain any amount of each other in their make up.
Secondary colours are made by mixing together any two primary colours:
  Red and yellow make orange
  Red and blue make violet
  Yellow and blue make green.
If all three primary colours are mixed together they produce tertiary colours. By altering the proportions of the mixture some interesting shades can be produced.
  Other useful colours are made by mixing together secondary neighbours, eg
  Yellow and orange make yellow-orange
  Orange and red make red-orange
  Red and violet make red-violet.

Twelve section colour-wheel   see page 60

This twelve section colour-wheel can be expanded many times but is usually satisfactory for most people's requirements.

Tints and shades

Tints and shades of a colour can be produced by adding various amounts of white or black to it. This can alter the character of the original colour. With the addition of white a colour becomes colder. Carmine is slightly bluish; yellow is less brilliant, blue, a cold colour already, alters very little and violet loses its masculine aggressiveness and becomes a pleasant lilac. Black added to green or violet can produce many attractive shades. Mixed with blue the blue soon disappears and yellow loses its brilliance and becomes murky.

Colour experiments

Interesting results can be created by mixing together certain colours. Professor Johannes Itten suggests these experiments:

1 Place any two colours at the ends of a strip. Mix them gradually.

2 Using the triangles, mix the two corner colours together. Then mix the three adjoining triangles to produce colours which are often difficult to name but attractive in a subtle sort of way.

3 Draw the square and divide it. Put four colours in the corners. Mix them gradually horizontally, vertically and diagonally.

Colours can be warm or cold. Yellows, oranges, reds and red-violets are usually considered warm, and greens, blues and blue-violets are cold. But this can change, depending on the colour next to it.

Colours can give an impression of depth. Dark colours seem to recede into a picture, while light colours advance. But the spatial effect can vary according to the depth of colour of the background. Yellow on black advances, but yellow on white recedes.

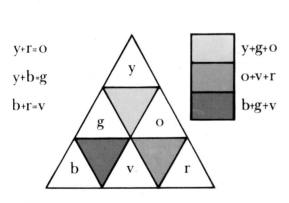

51 Colour experiments

Colour harmonies

Colour harmonies can be worked out in the following ways:

1 *Dyads* These are colours directly opposite each other on the colour wheel.

2 *Triads* These colours form an equilateral or isosceles triangle on the colour wheel.

3 *Tetrads* These combinations of four colours form a square or rectangle.

4 *Hexads* The six alternative colours of the 12-colour wheel are harmonious.

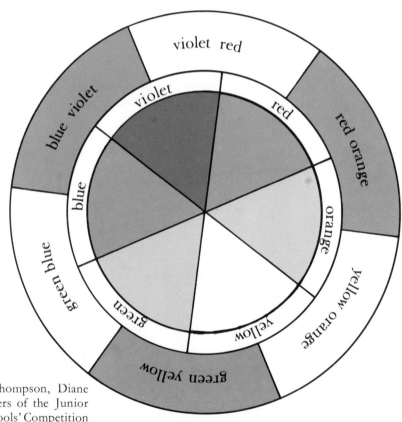

Facing page (left to right)
Designs by Janet Lockett, Susan Thompson, Diane
Gratty and Karen Stonehewer. Winners of the Junior
Section of the Embroiderers' Guild Schools' Competition
1969

60

52 Twelve section colour wheel

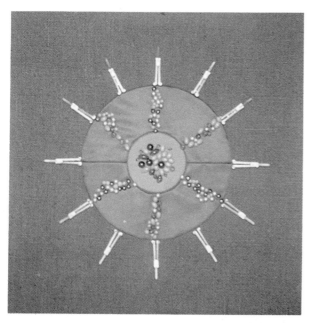
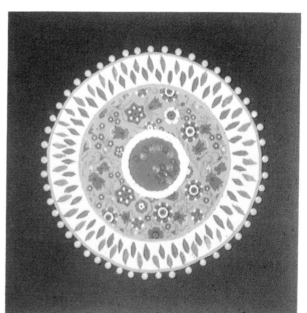

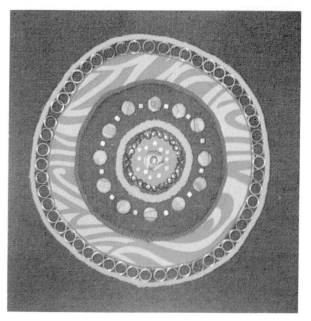

Colour balance

When choosing a colour scheme vary the tones so some colours are pure, some tints and some shades. Some colours are more dominant than others. Yellow on the colour wheel, where each colour is given the same amount of space, is brilliant compared with violet. Orange too, is brighter than blue. Red and green are comparable with each other. So if a balance of colour is required, more violet should be used than yellow, more blue than orange and equal amounts of red and green. It has been found that the following proportions give a balanced scheme:

$$\text{Yellow : violet} = \tfrac{1}{4} : \tfrac{3}{4}$$
$$\text{Orange : blue} = \tfrac{1}{3} : \tfrac{2}{3}$$
$$\text{Red \quad : green} = \tfrac{1}{2} : \tfrac{1}{2}$$

The colour balance wheel shows:

$$\text{Yellow : orange} = 3 : 4$$
$$\text{Yellow : red} = 3 : 6$$
$$\text{Yellow : violet} = 3 : 9$$
$$\text{Yellow : blue} = 3 : 8$$
$$\text{Yellow : green} = 3 : 6$$

When these ratios are altered, then the balance is changed and certain colours become dominant.

Contemporary colour schemes

These colour schemes are traditional but others can be found in contemporary art, etc which have become popular. At one time they would have been considered discordant, harsh and vulgar but familiarity has accustomed our eyes to them. These schemes rely on a change of tonal relationships. Traditionally a yellow would have been used which was lighter in tone than a violet. But today a darker yellow such as mustard would be used with a lighter violet like a pinky-lilac. Contemporary wallpapers, fabrics, carpets, etc provide examples of contemporary colour schemes. The *Anchor* cotton colour shade books are useful for seeing tones of a colour at a glance.

Collect examples of colour schemes from magazines of repute, save snippets of wallpaper patterns and samples of fabrics and threads.

Colour can be the inspiration for a panel. Certain topics can be visualised immediately in colour and translated into an abstract composition. Seasons have their own colours—Spring need not be a picture of daffodils and skipping lambs. It could be suggested by movement of line and, of course, choice of colours—yellows, white, pinks or blues with greens. Certain parts of the world have a dominant colour scheme—deserts, polar regions, jungles. Even regions in our own country vary colourwise depending on the surface rock and soil. Music can sometimes suggest mood, therefore colour. Nature is abundant in examples of colour schemes and flowers, insects and animals are often used as inspiration.

From the teacher's point of view, it is worthwhile to study colour to a greater depth than is covered in this chapter.

Suggestions for experiment

It is interesting to find out how fabrics become the colour they are. Sometimes on investigation, it is found that two or more colours are interwoven to give a particular colour effect. Advantage can be taken of this when withdrawing threads to create a design.

Experiment with transparent coloured fabrics. By superimposing one on another, a different colour can be produced.

Make abstract collages using a limited colour scheme.

Make a simple pictorial composition using tints, shades and the pure hue of one colour.

Experiment with harmony and discord.

Fabric colour can be obtained by printing and dying. This can be done in the classroom. Printing can be done with recognized or home-made tools.

Designs for tie-dying can be planned or not, depending on the choice of the individual. The printed or dyed fabric can be embroidered or decorated.

53 One of four embroidered tie-dye panels which were Commended in the 1969 Junior Section of the Embroiderers' Guild Schools Competition. The butterfly was first drawn on the fabric then parts of the wings were tied in bunches and the edges of the background were tied in pleats. After having been dyed, the wings were outlined with lace and stitches and beads were added
Caroline Barratt, Hill Top County Middle and Infants' School, Burslem

54 Multi-textured fabrics, mainly orange and red, make up this fabric collage
Terry Quinn, aged 7, Hill Top County Middle and Infants' School, Burslem

7 Texture

Texture is the word used to describe the surface of something. An awareness of texture is important in embroidery for embroidery is the decoration of a fabric with stitches or other fabrics, ie creating a new surface texture.

How the background is embellished depends on the properties of the fabric, the type of article to be embroidered and where it will be used. Fabrics vary in the density of their weave. Some are closely woven and stitches sewn with a fine cotton will still create a raised surface. Other fabrics are so loosely woven that some chunky stitches and beads can disappear from the surface into the holes. If one wishes to design and embroider a border for an apron, one would not expect the result to look the same as an embroidered border on a sumptuous evening skirt—the one has to be severely practical while the other need not be so. An embroidered wall panel to be viewed from a distance, eg at the end of a long corridor, will require a different type of technique from one meant to be seen at close range, eg in a living room. Small delicate detail on the former would be lost, but would be clearly visible on the latter.

Texture recognition

All fabrics and threads have their own textural properties. Net and chiffon are transparent. Hessian and evenweave linen are loosely woven. Plastic, leather and felt do not fray when cut. Satin and materials with metallic threads in them are shiny. Felt and flannel have a dull surface. Velvet and shot fabrics seem to change colour when turned in different directions. Satin and organdie are smooth but hessian is rough. Canvas is loosely woven but is stiffened to keep its shape. Threads can be thick or thin, hairy or smooth, shiny or dull, rounded or flat, elastic or taut, loosely stranded or tightly twisted.

Children delight in feeling fabrics. Arrange displays of articles which have a pronounced texture. Encourage the children to feel them. Quicken their ability to recognize textures by playing a 'touch' game. Blindfold a child, then hand her a piece of fabric to describe. A preliminary to this game could be recognizing when blindfolded, household articles with a definite texture. As well as naming the article, the child should describe its texture.

Collect and display fabrics of various textures. Experiment with different types of thread on different types of fabric.

Fabric construction and destruction

Fabrics can be made by various methods. Some are suitable as backgrounds, others could be used decoratively.

Simple patchwork, involving shapes easily sewn together by hand or machine can be utilised as a background for further decoration.

Fabrics can be woven. Various textures can be obtained depending on the threads used and the spacing between them.

Knitted fabrics can be used decoratively. A variety of textures can be made.

Crochet work can be attached to a fabric to embellish it.

Knotting together a number of threads produces an openweave fabric.

The surface of a fabric can be altered by other means than adding to it. Pushing aside threads of an open-weave fabric creates a new texture.

Pulling out certain threads and combinations of threads alters the surface texture.

A combination of pulling, pushing and tying is possible.

Cutting holes is another way of changing the fabric.

Fraying creates loose threads of predetermined length which can be worked in a number of ways.

Surface texture can be acquired by gathering, rolling, pleating and padding.

Beads, sequins and other odds and ends add texture to a background fabric.

Stitches, whether they are simple, looped, knotted or composite give texture of varying depth depending on the type of weave of the background and the thickness of thread.

As well as using ready-made fabrics and threads, it is interesting to use some made by yourself. Threads can be made by twisting, plaiting, knotting and looping. Lengths of cut fabric, and threads pulled from a woven fabric can be used. Very thick threads can be couched to the surface with the possibility of only entering the fabric at the beginning and end of a length.

When designing, remember to allow for textured areas. They should be in proportion to the whole. Too much of the same sort of texture would tend to cancel itself out.

Light direction has an effect on texture. If the source of light varies from place to place during the day, eg sunlight from a window, directed light from a spotlight, evening light from a central ceiling fitment—a textured wall panel design will seem to be continually changing because of the shadows being cast in different directions.

To summarize, fabrics and threads can be of very different textures. Home-made threads can be constructed by twisting, plaiting, knotting and looping. Fabrics can be constructed from patchwork, and by weaving, knitting, crochetting and knotting. Fabric destruction by pulling, tying and fraying alters a piece of material. Surface change through gathering, rolling, pleating and padding is possible. Finally, stitches, beads, sequins, rings, washers, buttons, etc all decorate the fabric and if used in the right place for the right purpose will produce effective texture.

56 Woven orange velvet ribbon, raised chain band stitch and jet buckles on a woollen fabric background Anne Butler

Facing page
57 *Move* Anne Butler. Applied fabric and stitches create contrasting areas of texture on the background fabric

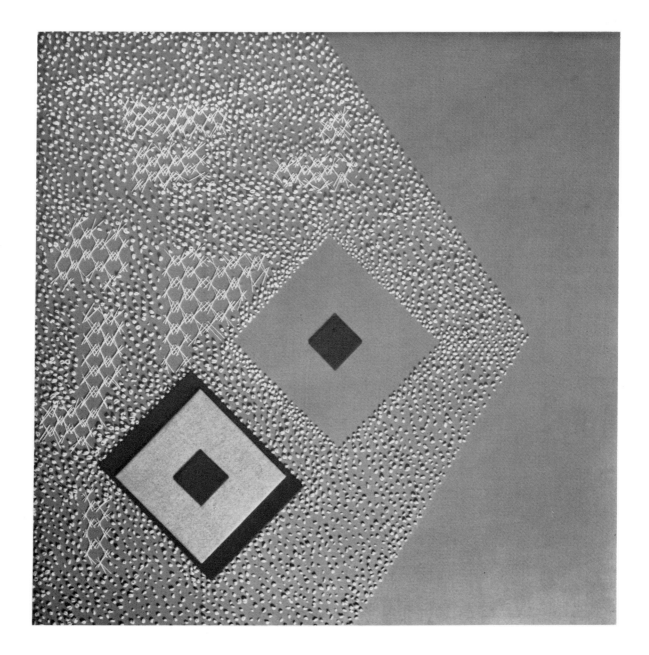

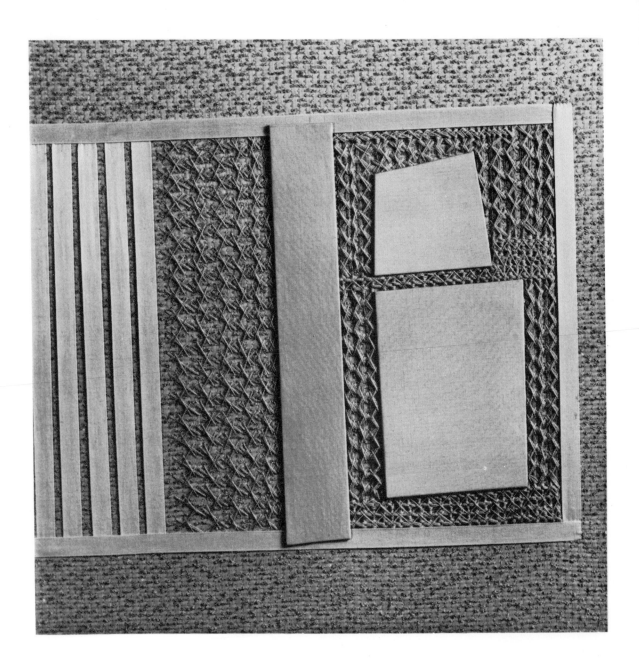

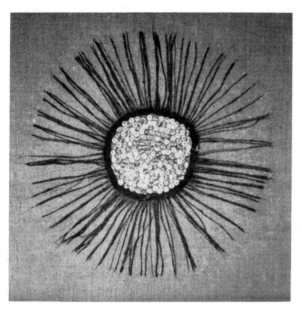

59 A length of hessian was frayed and made into a circle to represent a multi-petalled flower. The centre was filled with chunky beads
Beverley Hood, Hill Top County Middle and Infants' School, Burslem

Facing page
58 *In Blue* Anne Butler. Applied ribbons separate a textured background from areas of applied fabric shapes and stitches

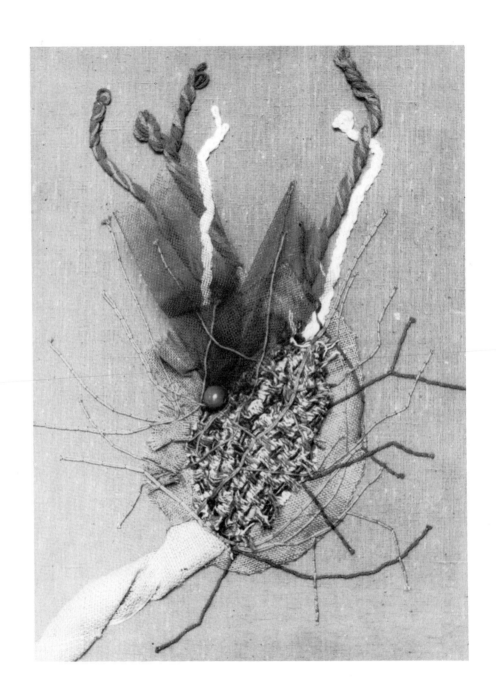

60 *Love-in-a-mist*
Dorothy Gandevia,
Australia

Facing page
61   *Shadow Trees*
Mary Goldizen, USA

8 Some methods of creating designs

Apart from simplifying and adapting subjects, there are other methods of designing which are not only suitable for use in schools but also are useful for mature work.

Some designs created by the following methods can be planned, but others are accidental. Teachers and children, trying these methods for the first time, can be disappointed with the results, but they are so easy and quick to do that many experiments can be produced in a short time and out of these the best can be selected for the particular purpose in mind.

I am continually surprised by the variety of designs children are capable of producing. One day when we were designing with cut paper, the end of the afternoon came upon us suddenly. Our exploded circles, which we had meticulously cut up, had to be stored away until the next lesson. When we came to reassemble them, it was almost impossible to find their original positions so it was suggested that we abandon our original idea and assemble the pieces in whatever shape we liked. Some children were inspired by the particular shape of one piece and they followed up the idea, creating an astonishing variety of forms.

Sometimes children do not know when their designs are finished and they will spoil a satisfactory piece of work by continuing to cut out more shapes or by adding more paint. If the teacher can work with a group rather than a class then she can supervise its activities and suggest tactfully when enough has been done. This applies particularly to work with paint. Some attractive results can be obtained by dropping one blob of paint onto a larger one and leaving them to merge and run at will. The over-enthusiastic will want to add further colours and will want to tilt the paper to encourage the merger and will finish up with a muddy coloured mess. So restraint has to be taught!

Foreground and background design

The designs produced by the following suggested methods can be of primary or secondary importance. That is, they can be the subject matter or the background. Their role in a composition depends on the embroidery method used and the colours and textures involved. In canvas work, for instance, where the background may be required to be worked to complete the panel, a seemingly complicated design can be worked without detracting from the subject matter. Choose colours and textures which are a contrast to the subject. If the colours chosen are mostly of similar density, that is, mostly light or medium or dark, then the resulting background will have unity. Changes in stitch and type of thread will also add further interest without detracting attention from the subject matter.

Doodling

Doodling can produce interesting designs which can be used in embroidery. From experience I have found that the best doodles for this purpose are drawn without premeditation. My son likes to design, but if I suggest to him that he draws something for me, his inspiration dries up! On the other hand his doodles, drawn it seems without thought, while watching the television perhaps, sometimes accompanied by snatches of song, other times by noises resembling gunfire, can be very interesting! These are the ones I find myself putting into my scrapbook for future reference.

Cut paper

Cut paper is a traditional method of designing for embroidery. Scraps can be arranged in a pleasing manner. Similar or different geometrical or free shapes may be assembled to create a design. Using tissue paper shapes gives tonal variations when they overlap and colour changes when more than one colour of paper is used.

Squares, circles, rectangles, diamonds, etc can be folded any number of times and shapes cut out of them.

Large squares, rectangles and diamonds of white paper can be divided with pencil lines into numerous smaller squares, rectangles and diamonds, then cut along these lines and stuck onto a piece of black paper, the same size as the original white one.

A design cut out of half a white square can be stuck onto a black background at the left-hand side while the remaining part of the rectangle is stuck onto the right-hand side of the black square.

A folded geometric shape may be cut on the edges not folded and the pieces turned over onto the background. Or the shapes can be cut out of the folded edge, slit along the fold and placed opposite the hole at each side.

Exploded shapes can be stuck down on a contrasting background. The resulting outline can be similar to the original shape or different. The shapes can be completely re-arranged as earlier suggested.

A free design can be created by first cutting out curved lines then cutting out shapes from the solid areas.

Figures, too, can be made from cut paper, either singly or in strips.

Cut fabric

Another method of designing connected with cutting is to cut out motifs from a patterned fabric and arrange them in a new design. The children did this when they worked at Christmas time panels of each of the Three Kings, one of which is illustrated in figure 39. They cut out flower and leaf motifs from a furnishing fabric, arranged them at the sides of the kings and couched them down with wool. In two instances the kings' robes were also decorated with cut-out motifs.

When designing the masks (page 80), use was made of the patterns of the fabrics to emphasise a particular line or shape.

Rubbings

Rubbings of any textured surface give interesting designs suitable for background in canvas work. The patterns can also be used to fill shapes or areas with surface stitches. Bark and rock rubbings are those most often used, but many household objects and items of school equipment will produce a pattern when rubbed with heelball on paper.

Printing

Designs from printing with many types of tools, factory-made and home-made, can have accidental variations in texture. Found objects, like stones, empty boxes, lids and natural objects such as flowers, leaves, grasses and sections of fruit and vegetables make useful printing tools. They can be mounted on a block of wood or a roller to be used, or they can be painted then sandwiched between two sheets of paper and pressed.

Paint designs

'Accidental' designs are produced by a number of means using water paint or coloured inks. 'Splash' patterns are made by splashing any number of colours onto the paper. On a large scale this can be done by a group on the floor. As an extra, the wet surface can be combed in various directions.

Solar Night   Joy Clucas

Winter   Joy Clucas

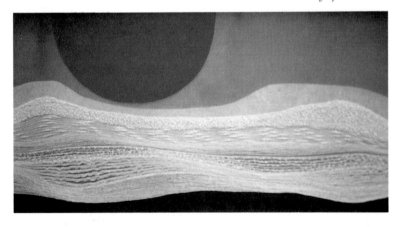

Paint or ink blowing and folded paper blobs often result in shapes like forms in nature, the blown ink resembling trees in winter or spider-like insects and the blobs looking like butterflies or beetles.

String, striped with various colours of paint, pressed between two sheets of paper and pulled in an arc, makes a design.

Marbling using oil and paint can make interesting patterns.

My favourite method of designing using paint is wet paint blending. Many experiments can be done and not only are individual designs made but new colours are found. The idea is simply to drop blobs of paint on top of each other and watch the results. The blobs can vary in size and shape and the number of colours used depends on the choice of the individual, but it is a good idea to limit the number of colours, especially to the over-enthusiastic.

Experiment with:

Warm colours and one neutral

Cool colours and one neutral

Two adjoining colours on the colour wheel and one neutral

Primary colours

Dyads, eg yellow and violet

Triads, eg yellow, blue and red

Tetrads, eg green, orange, red and blue

Hexads, eg yellow, orange, red, violet, blue and green.

Many other methods of designing can be found in books devoted solely to that subject. (See *Bibliography*.)

62   Re-arranged pieces from an exploded circle
Kevin Findler, Hill Top County Middle and Infants'
School, Burslem

63 *Moon turning Blue* Joy Clucas. This type of design can be created from an exploded shape

64 'Splash' pattern

65 *Inferno* Joy Clucas. This type of design can originate from merging paint blobs or layers of cut tissue paper stuck on top of each other

66 and 67 Patterned fabric was deliberately chosen to emphasise certain features on these masks
Sheila Oakes and Lynn Shaw, Hill Top County Middle and Infants' School, Burslem

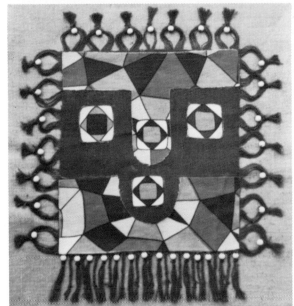

68 One of four bird collages which were Highly Commended in the 1969 Junior Section of the Embroiderers' Guild Schools' Competition
Karen Bloor, Hill Top County Middle and Infants' School, Burslem

9 Equipment and techniques

Fabrics and threads

Schools are limited in what they can buy in the way of fabrics and threads, etc, by the contents of the various schools' suppliers catalogues. Hessian, net, cottons, linens, organdie and felt are available from these suppliers but the quality of the fabrics varies. The traditional types of threads are readily available but are often expensive. Some weaving cottons work out cheaper than the soft embroidery type and ordinary knitting wool can be less expensive than tapestry wool.

So teachers rely on what they can obtain from other sources. We receive bits and pieces from parents and friends. My hairdresser, who has an eye for beautiful fabrics, gives us the scraps left over from her evening dresses. A travelling acquaintance on the bus, when she heard of our work, offered to give us waste from the clothing factory where she works. Other local factories willingly give us scraps which would otherwise be thrown away.

Sizeable samples of fabrics can be bought in shops at a very reasonable price. Smaller samples can sometimes be obtained from mills and remnants bought cheaply from markets and in sales. Sometimes a garment can be bought at a jumble sale to be cut up, but make sure the fabric is in good condition.

Threads, too, can often be acquired from various sources. Wool bought from the mill is cheaper than that in the shops. Our school nurse brought us a big bag of old wools which had belonged to her mother. They were of a quality not found today. She also gave us a box of old buttons. It was like sorting through a treasure chest going through that box. There were some beautiful buttons in it. Some were like brooches; they were so intricate. Tiny sleeve buttons and shoe buttons were a delight to the eye.

All types of fabrics and threads can be used in embroidery, whether they are of natural origin like those made from cotton, linen, wool, silk and jute or man-made like nylon, terylene, rayon and plastic. Furnishing fabrics and materials from dress fabrics departments are all suitable. More unusual materials such as leather or suede can be incorporated. Backgrounds need not be restricted to hessian. Many furnishing fabrics, heavy cotton, linen and woollen dress fabrics can be used successfully, the weave or combination of colours adding interest.

Anything which can be threaded through the eye of a needle or couched onto the surface can be used as a thread. Wools, cottons and strings can be obtained in a variety of thicknesses. Raffene, ribbon, plastic wire, chenille, candlewick and metal threads produce interesting effects.

Beads

Beads, sequins, buttons, mirror discs, curtain rings, braids, pieces of coloured acetate and other odds and ends from hardware stores and haberdashery departments may be added to the background to create areas of texture. Embroidery beads are sometimes rather small for children to use but broken necklaces are useful. These necklaces can be bought cheaply in multiple stores and markets. Wooden beads in a variety of shapes, sizes and colours can be bought from schools' suppliers.

Needles and scissors

A good supply of sewing needles of various types should always be available. Knitting needles and crochet hooks are a useful addition.

Scissors should be sharp and kept for embroidery if possible. Paper cutting blunts them.

Adhesives

The cellulose type of adhesive, such as *Polycell*, is suitable for most types of fabric, but impact glue (*Evo-stik*) and *PVA* are useful for heavier fabrics.

Frames

Some designs are easier to work if they are framed. Slate frames are expensive but a cheap one can be made to size by joining four pieces of wood with angle irons. Attach the fabric to this with staples.

Mounting

The finished work should be neatly mounted. A cheap way of doing this is to stretch it over stiff card and lace it at the back, mitring the corners. Another cheap way is to leave it on the wooden frame and fit another one round the edge. Existing picture frames can be utilized, of course.

Before mounting, the work sometimes needs to be pulled into shape. This applies particularly to canvas work, although working on a frame helps to keep the canvas true. To straighten the work it should be dampened, pulled and pinned to a correctly shaped board and left to dry to the correct measurements.

Stitches

Stitches and methods of embroidery can sometimes be taught incidentally and at other times definite short exercises using a particular stitch or method can be worked. Experiment with a stitch, using different types of thread on different types of fabrics and notice the resulting effects for future use. Alter the size and direction of the stitch, work a number of them close together in groups or in short, close rows. Build up a collection of these experiments and exercises, mount them and label them giving details of stitch or method, thread and fabric. Books giving details of stitches and methods or simple instruction cards for younger children should be available for reference. Any stitch in the recognised groups—flat, looped, chained, knotted and composite—can be attempted. Some methods are easier to work than others but older and more capable children may want to try the more difficult methods. Appliqué, blackwork, canvas work, couching, drawn fabric, drawn thread, needleweaving, net embroidery and patchwork are within the capabilities of older children and can be attempted in small amounts by younger children.

Collage

Fabric collage is now recognised as a method and it is a valuable one to introduce to young children. They welcome the ease and speed of applying adhesive to the fabrics. The adhesive can be applied all over the back or in a certain spot depending on the required effect. The cock's feathers in illustration 68 were only partially stuck down to give depth to the bird.

Displays and exhibitions

Exhibitions of modern embroidery panels and hangings are held in various parts of the country and displays of traditional work can be seen in local museums. The teacher who is a member of the Embroiderers' Guild can borrow portfolios of work, coloured transparencies of traditional and contemporary work and books on all aspects of embroidery.

Being able to see the works of other people, whether they are by children, students, amateurs or artist-craftsmen, whether the work is traditional or contemporary, is part of children's education. By using their eyes they become aware of how points, lines and shapes with the addition of colour and texture can be arranged into a pleasing composition, and how fabrics, threads and sundries can be used to interpret the design.

Bibliography

Design in Embroidery Kathleen Whyte Batsford London and Branford
  Newton Centre Massachusetts

Inspiration for Embroidery Constance Howard Batsford London and
  Branford Newton Centre Massachusetts

Embroidery and Fabric Collage Eirian Short Pitman London and Drake
  Publishing Company New York

Canvas Embroidery Diana Springall Batsford London and Branford
  Newton Centre Massachusetts

Ideas for Canvas Work Mary Rhodes Batsford London and Branford
  Newton Centre Massachusetts

Creative Textile Craft: Thread and Fabric Rolf Hartung Batsford London
  and Van Nostrand Reinhold New York

Introducing Patchwork Alice Timmins Batsford London and Watson-
  Guptill New York (now out of print)

Introducing Fabric Collage Margaret Connor Batsford London and
  Watson-Guptill New York

Embroidery Book Mary Thomas Hodder and Stoughton London and
  William Morrow New York

Dictionary of Embroidery Stitches Mary Thomas Hodder and Stoughton
  London and William Morrow New York

Pattern and Embroidery Anne Butler and David Green Batsford London
  and Branford Newton Centre Massachusetts

Simple Stitches Anne Butler Batsford London and Praeger New York

Creative Drawing; Point and Line Röttger Batsford London and Van
  Nostrand Reinhold New York

150 Techniques in Art Hans Meyers Batsford London and Van Nostrand
  Reinhold New York

Graphic Design Manual Armin Hofmann Alec Tiranti London

Abstract Pictures on Film Hajek-Halke Dennis Dobson London and
  Viking Press Inc New York

Structure in Art and Science Gyorgy Kepes Studio Vista London and
  George Braziller New York

The New Landscape in Art and Science Gyorgy Kepes Alec Tiranti London
  and Paul Theobald Chicago

The Nature of Art and Motion   Gyorgy Kepes   Studio Vista London and George Braziller New York

Module, Symmetry and Proportion   Gyorgy Kepes   Studio Vista London and George Braziller New York

Surfaces in Creative Design   Röttger/Klante   Batsford London and Van Nostrand Reinhold New York

Designing with String   Mary Seyd   Batsford London and Watson-Guptill New York

Creative Rubbings   Laye Andrew   Batsford London and Watson-Guptill New York

Suppliers

Great Britain

Fabrics, threads and all embroidery accessories

Fred Aldous Limited   The Handicraft Centre   PO Box 135   37 Lever Street   Manchester   M60 1UX
Arts and Crafts   10 Byram Street   Huddersfield   HD1 1DA
Art Needlework Industries Limited   7 St Michael's Mansions   Ship Street   Oxford
Harrods Limited   Brompton Road   London SW1
Mace and Nairn   Crane Street   Salisbury   Wiltshire
The Needlewoman Shop   Regent Street   London W1
Nottingham Handcraft Company   Melton Road   West Bridgford   Nottingham
Louis Grossé Limited   36 Manchester Street   London W1

Beads

The Bead Shop   South Molton Street   London W1
Sesame Ventures   New Invention   Dulverton   Somerset
Ells and Farrier   5 Princes Street   London W1

Leather

The Light Leather Company   16 Soho Square   London W1

USA

American Thread Corporation   90 Park Avenue   New York NY
Bucky King Embroideries Unlimited   121 South Drive   Pittsburgh   Pensylvania 15238
Hollander Bead and Novelty Corporation   25 West 37 Street   New York 18 NY
The Needle's Point Studio   1626 Macon Street   McLean   Virginia 22101
Yarn Depot   Sutter Street   San Francisco 94102